WHAT IS A THEOCRACY?

SARAH B. BOYLE

Crabtree Publishing Company

www.crabtreebooks.com

Crabtree Publishing Company
www.crabtreebooks.com

Produced and developed by Netscribes Inc.

Author: Sarah B. Boyle
Publishing plan research and development:
Sean Charlebois, Reagan Miller
Crabtree Publishing Company
Editors: Valerie J. Weber
Proofreader: Wendy Scavuzzo
Art director: Dibakar Acharjee
Picture researcher: Sandeep Kumar Guthikonda
Project coordinator: Kathy Middleton
Production coordinator: Kenneth J. Wright
Prepress technician: Margaret Amy Salter
Cover design: Margaret Amy Salter and Katherine Berti
Print coordinator: Katherine Berti

Front cover: Pope Francis I (front left) is the leader of the Vatican City (background); A statue of Buddha (top inset); Justice Agha Rafiq Ahmed Khan (Chief Justice, Federal Shariat Court of Pakistan) (bottom inset)

Title page: Iran's supreme leader, Ayatollah Ali Khamenei deliv

Photographs:

Title page: BEHROUZ MEHRI/AFP/Getty Images; P4: Casa Rosada/Wikimedia Commons; P5: Dmitri Ometsinsky/Shutterstock; P6: Arno Burgi/dpa/Corbis; P7: Asianet-Pakistan/Shutterstock; P8-9: Mart/Shutterstock; P10: Mirek Hejnicki/Shutterstock; P11: Libor Piska/Shutterstock; P12: Bettmann/CORBIS; P13: rafalex/Shutterstock; P14: ruskpp/Shutterstock; P15: mountainpix/Shutterstock; P16: Scheufler Collection/CORBIS; P17: Asianet-Pakistan/Shutterstock; P18: AFP/Getty Images; P19: MOHAMMED HUWAIS/AFP/Getty Images; P20: ROBYN BECK/AFP/Getty Images; P21: Graham arrison/arabianEye/Corbis; P22: Liang Youchang/Xinhua Press/Corbis; P23.1: Hulton Archive/Stringer; P23.2: vipflash / Shutterstock; P24: Imagno/Getty Images; P25: Thomas Trutschel/Photothek via Getty Images; P26: SHAH MARAI/AFP/Getty Images; P27: Stringer/AFP/Getty Images; P28: Volina/Shutterstock; P29: MOHAMMED HUWAIS/AFP/Getty Images; P30: ATTA KENARE/AFP/Getty Images; P31: AFP/Getty Images; P32: Nickolay Vinokurov/Shutterstock; P33: STRINGER/AFP/Getty Images; P34: FAYEZ URELDINE/AFP/Getty Images; P35: Kaveh Kazemi/Getty Images; P36: PENGYOU91/Shutterstock; P37: Rahhal/Shutterstock; P40: Bettmann/CORBIS; P41: McCarthy's PhotoWorks / Shutterstock; P42: Attila JANDI/Shutterstock; P43: huafeng207/ Shutterstock; P44.1: ayzek/Shutterstock; P44.2: pavalena/Shutterstock; P45: Vepar5/Shutterstock.Wikimedia Commons: Gryffindor: cover (inset, statue); Wikimedia Commons: Aghaharis: cover (inset bottom); zumapress.com/Keystonepress: cover (Pope); all other images by Shutterstock.

Library and Archives Canada Cataloguing in Publication

Boyle, Sarah B., 1981-
    What is a theocracy? / Sarah B. Boyle.

(Forms of government)
Includes index.
Issued also in electronic format.
ISBN 978-0-7787-5319-3 (bound).--ISBN 978-0-7787-5326-1 (pbk.)

    1. Theocracy--Juvenile literature. I. Title. II. Series: Forms of government (St. Catharines, Ont.)

JC372.B69 2013   j321'.5   C2013-901029-7

Library of Congress Cataloging-in-Publication Data

Boyle, Sarah B., 1981-
    What is a theocracy? / Sarah B. Boyle.
      pages cm -- (Forms of government)
    Includes index.
    ISBN 978-0-7787-5319-3 (reinforced library binding) -- ISBN 978-0-7787-5326-1 (pbk.) -- ISBN 978-1-4271-8790-1 (electronic pdf) -- ISBN 978-1-4271-9628-6 (electronic html)
    1. Theocracy--Juvenile literature. I. Title.

JC372.B69 2013
321'.5--dc23
                                        2013004911

Crabtree Publishing Company

Printed in the U.S.A./042013/SX20130306

www.crabtreebooks.com   1-800-387-7650

Published in Canada
Crabtree Publishing
616 Welland Ave.
St. Catharines, Ontario
L2M 5V6

Published in the United States
Crabtree Publishing
PMB 59051
350 Fifth Avenue, 59th Floor
New York, New York 10118

Published in the United Kingdom
Crabtree Publishing
Maritime House
Basin Road North, Hove
BN41 1WR

Published in Australia
Crabtree Publishing
3 Charles Street
Coburg North
VIC 3058

CONTENTS

THEOCRACY: THE BASICS

A government is made up of people who organize and manage a country. Governments are responsible for creating and enforcing laws. They also provide important services for their citizens.

What Is a Theocracy?

A theocracy is one of many forms of government. In a theocracy, the people who run the government are tied to the church. A church is an organized group of people who all follow the same religion. In a theocracy, the church and government are not separate. Both **institutions** organize and manage the country. Laws are based directly on religious beliefs or the church's policies.

In 2013, Francis I became pope. The pope is the head of the Catholic Church and the leader of Vatican City, which is a theocracy.

Constitution

A constitution states the basic beliefs and laws that govern a country. It describes who has power and how they can use that power. All laws a country passes must agree with the constitution. If a law goes against what a constitution states, that law has no force. In a theocracy, the constitution is usually based on religious laws.

A form of **Christianity**, the Eastern Orthodox Church is Greece's state religion. However, Greek laws are not based on the rules of the Eastern Orthodox Church.

Governed by God

In ancient times, the leaders of a theocracy were often believed to be gods. The people believed that their leader had **supernatural** powers. They worshipped their leader because they believed he had power over life, death, and the natural world. They usually did whatever he asked of them.

Not all leaders govern as gods. Some countries' leaders rule because they have a direct connection with their religion's god. They claim to know what a god wants because the god has spoken directly to them. The people in these theocracies follow the leaders because they also want to do what their god wants.

An ecclesiocracy is a kind of theocracy in which the leaders of a church are also the leaders of the government. They are not gods and do not have a direct connection to god. But they rule the country based on the rules of their god and religion.

State Religion and Theocracy

A state religion is the official religion of a country. It is legally approved by its government. The government may even give money to support the religion. Some governments do not allow any religion besides the state religion. Others allow other religions but do not officially support them.

Countries that have a state religion are not always theocracies. For example, Greece's state religion is the Eastern Orthodox Church of Greece. However, Greece is a democracy. For a government to be a theocracy, the laws of the religion must be the laws of the entire country.

A Modern Theocracy

Most theocracies in the world today are in **Muslim** countries, or nations that practice the religion of **Islam**. Saudi Arabia, in the Middle East, is one such country. In Islam, the Quran is the holiest book. *Sharia* is the term for the laws of the religion. Saudi Arabia does not have an independent constitution to base its laws on. Instead, the country uses the Quran and sharia law as a constitution. There are no laws in Saudi Arabia except for the religious laws of Islam.

The King and the Royal Family

Saudi Arabia's king is in charge of the government. All kings are members of the royal family. The king issues royal **decrees**, which tell the government how to operate. The king is also in charge of **appointing** all other members of government. All regional governors and the heads of important government departments are members of the royal family. The royal family and the king do not have total power, though. Like their citizens, they must follow sharia law and the Quran.

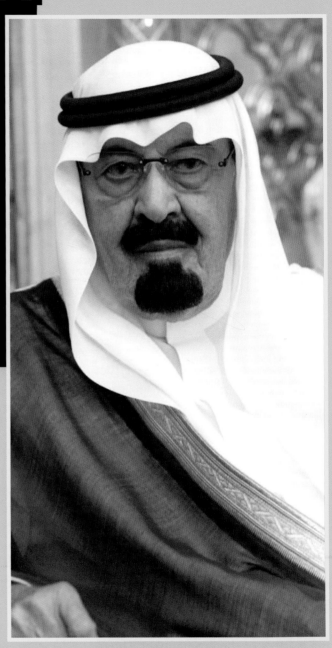

King Abdullah is the leader of Saudi Arabia. He became king after his brother died in 2005.

The ulema has a direct role in government
It must approve all laws in Saudi Arabia.

Two Powerful Families

The royal family is the most powerful
group of people in Saudi Arabia. But
another important family also helps rule
the government. This family is made up
of the country's religious leaders. The
members of this family make up the *ulema*.
The ulema are a group of Islamic religious
leaders and scholars. Any decisions the
king makes must be approved by the
ulema. The ulema must also approve
of the appointment of a new king.

The royal family and the family that make
up the ulema made an agreement 300 years
ago. The royal family agreed to support the
leading religious family's power in the
religion of Saudi Arabia. And the religious
family agreed to support the royal family's
power in the government of Saudi Arabia.

The Laws of Islam

The laws of Islam are the supreme laws
of Saudi Arabia. The government and
the church work together to enforce the
rules of Islam. The government makes and
enforces laws based on Islam. The ulema
interpret these laws. And the citizens of
Saudi Arabia must follow these laws.

A Religious Education

Muslims believe a good
education is necessary to
understanding Islam. Ulema
members spend years
studying Islam. At the end
of their studies, they
receive a degree in
Islamic law.

THEOCRACIES OF THE WORLD

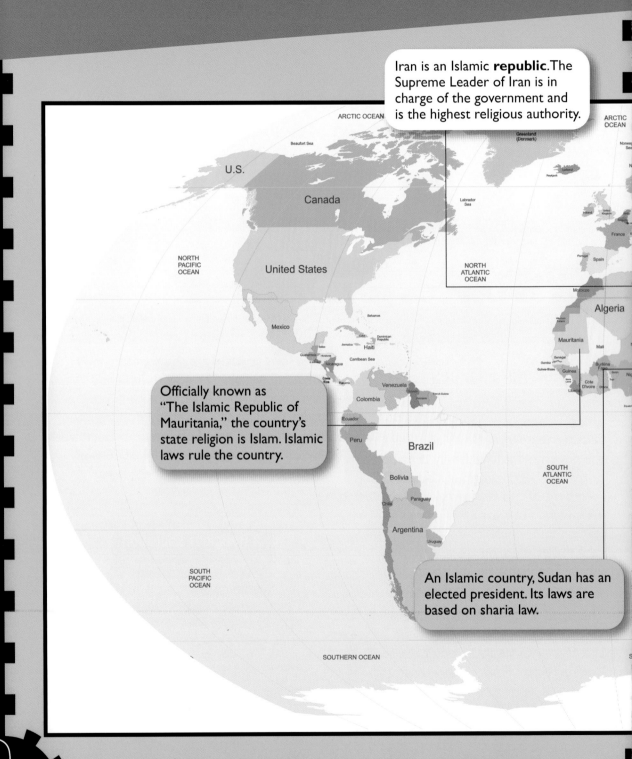

Iran is an Islamic **republic**. The Supreme Leader of Iran is in charge of the government and is the highest religious authority.

Officially known as "The Islamic Republic of Mauritania," the country's state religion is Islam. Islamic laws rule the country.

An Islamic country, Sudan has an elected president. Its laws are based on sharia law.

Vatican City is the smallest independent state in the world. The pope is head of the government and head of the Catholic Church.

Afghanistan's constitution declares it an "Islamic Republic." All laws are based on the laws of Islam.

The people elect Yemen's president and legislature. Laws are based on sharia law and enforced by an Islamic judicial branch.

After a **civil war**, Somalia is becoming a democracy. Islamic law forms the basis of its laws and judicial system.

The Quran and sharia law are the basis of the government of Saudi Arabia. It is an Islamic theocracy.

Theocracy is as old as the written word. Early theocracies were based on emperors and pharaohs who were believed to be gods. Theocracies then became governments where religious leaders were in charge of the Church and the government. Theocracies are now governments that base their laws on religious laws.

Ancient Theocracy

Many ancient civilizations were theocracies. Leaders of the governments were worshipped as gods. The people often believed in many gods. The leader of the theocracy was one of these gods. The people believed he could communicate with the other gods. They wanted him to bless their crops or bring rain to dry fields. So they offered him sacrifices by killing animals or even other people.

The pharaohs, or kings, of ancient Egypt ruled from 3000 BCE to about 30 BCE. The people of Egypt worshipped the pharaohs as some of their gods. The gods were responsible for sunrise, sunset, life, death, the Nile River, and other parts of the natural world. They followed the wishes of the pharaoh. In return, he would ask the other gods to make sure the world worked smoothly.

Akhenaten was pharaoh of Egypt from 1352 to 1336 BCE.

Theocracy in the Americas

Halfway around the world from Egypt, the Mayans of Central America had a similar theocracy. From 250 to 900 CE, the kings of the Mayan **city-states** ruled over theocratic governments. Like the Egyptians, the Mayans believed in many gods that controlled the natural world. They worshipped their kings alongside these other gods.

But the Mayans' worship was extreme. The Mayan religion demanded that its followers sacrifice people to the gods. They fought wars to capture warriors and sometimes other kings to sacrifice to the gods. The people often cut themselves to offer their own blood to the gods as well. In return, they believed the gods gave them good harvests and kept their civilization alive.

The Mayans also built large stepped pyramids. These pyramids often had religious temples at the top. They were used as places for worship and sacrifice. Sometimes kings were buried in the pyramids because they were considered gods.

The Benin Empire

During that time, powerful monarchs also existed in Asia, Africa, and the Middle East. A major monarchy in Africa, the Benin Empire began in the 1300s and existed until 1897. The Benin Empire became wealthy in part by trading with the Europeans. The powerful monarch, called an oba, lived in an extravagant palace in the kingdom's capital, Benin City. By the 1600s, the empire stretched across a major portion of western Africa.

Rebuilding the Pyramids

The Mayans rebuilt the pyramids about every 50 years. Historians believe they rebuilt them when a new ruler took over. He wanted to prove his power as a god and required these religious buildings be remade to his liking.

3000 BCE	First pharaoh ruled in ancient Egypt, a theocracy
30 BCE	End of the pharaohs' rule in Egypt
250–900 CE	Mayan city-states run by kings who are worshipped as gods

Rules from God

As theocracies developed, religious leaders and **prophets** governed larger and larger groups of people. They stopped behaving like gods themselves. They now ruled based on messages they received from God. These messages gave the rules people should live by.

Islamic Theocracies

Islamic theocracies date back to the beginning of the Islamic religion. A prophet, Muhammad founded Islam in 622 CE. Muhammad was said to have written down what God told him in the Koran. Muhammad then founded the first Islamic state in Medina in present-day Saudi Arabia. He governed based on the Koran's rules. Muhammad united the independent tribes of the Arabian Peninsula under Islam.

Islamic Caliphs

A caliph is the ruler of an Islamic state. Caliphs are believed to be direct **descendants** of Muhammad. Abdülmecid II was the last caliph. He ruled the **Ottoman Empire** before World War I, which began in 1914. After the Ottoman Empire collapsed in 1923, there were no more caliphs.

Abdülmecid II was the last in a series of caliphs who ruled the Muslim world.

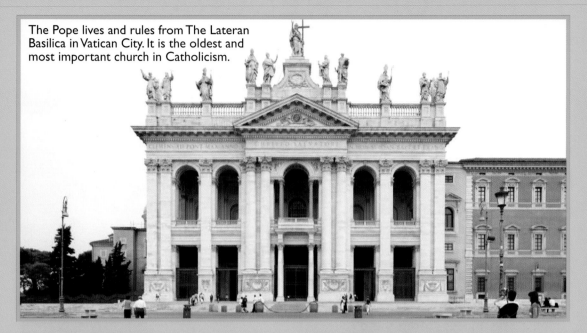

The Pope lives and rules from The Lateran Basilica in Vatican City. It is the oldest and most important church in Catholicism.

Christian Theocracy

Around the same time, a Christian theocracy was developing in Europe. In 754 CE, the Catholic Church officially created the Papal States. The Papal States were a collection of governments in Italy that were governed by the pope. The pope did not have a direct link to the Catholic god. But his **interpretation** of Catholicism is infallible, which means he cannot be wrong. The pope ruled as the leader of the Church and the government until 1870, when Italy took over the Papal States. Today the pope remains the head of a theocracy, but it is limited to Vatican City in Italy.

Iran: A Modern Theocracy

The leaders of modern theocracies do not have a special link to god that allows them to rule. But they are considered experts on their religion. The leader of Iran is called the Supreme Leader. In 1979, Iran approved a constitution that made its government a theocracy. All laws would be based on the laws of Islam. The Supreme Leader's job is to make sure the government follows these laws. The Supreme Leader must be able to interpret the laws of Islam and apply them to his rule of the country.

622	Muhammad founded the religion of Islam and ruled a theocracy in the Arabian Peninsula
632–1923	Series of caliphs ruled Islamic countries in and around the Arabian Peninsula
754	Catholic Church founded Papal States
754–1870	Pope ruled as leader of Catholic Church and the government of the Papal States
1979–present	Iran is ruled as a modern theocracy

Theocracy comes in many forms. In the earliest theocracies, the head of the government was a god.

Ruled by God

The God of the Hebrew Bible could be described as a theocratic ruler. The **Jewish** people lived their lives according to the laws of God. Between 1500 and 1300 BCE, God gave the Ten Commandments, or rules, to a prophet named Moses. Moses shared these rules with the other Jews. They followed all God's laws faithfully.

Theocracies can also be ruled by a prophet who tells the people what God wants. The prophet Muhammad led the Muslims because he had a direct link to God.

Moses holds the Ten Commandments, ten laws that God gave directly to him.

Ecclesiocracy

In another form of theocracy, the person in charge of the Church is also in charge of the government. In an ecclesiocracy, the leader is not a god and does not have a direct link with god. But he rules the country based on the rules of the Church. If there is a conflict between the Church and the government, the Church always wins.

Vatican City

Vatican City is a walled city-state inside the city of Rome, Italy. It covers a little more than 100 acres (2 sq km). Its population is just over 800 people. It is a theocracy and the smallest independent state in the world.

Caesaropapism

Another variation on theocracy is called caesaropapism. In caesaropapism, the government has more power than the Church. There are often two leaders: one in charge of the government and one in charge of the Church. An emperor or king controls the government. And the Church is run by its own leader. The Church and its leader have to follow the commands of the emperor or king.

A caesaropapist government ruled the **Byzantine Empire**. The Byzantine emperors had almost complete control over the Eastern Christian Church from 330 CE to the 900s. In fights over property, the government protected the Church's interests. In exchange, the emperor had control over the Church's great wealth and property. It also used the Church to pass laws and **edicts**, then to enforce them.

Blended Theocracies

Today theocracies are often blended with republics and democracies. Their constitutions are based on the rules of the religion. But the citizens of the country elect the officials who run the government. These officials are then responsible for following the constitution and enforcing the laws of the religion.

Justinian I ruled the Byzantine Empire from 527 to 565 CE. He worked to create religious unity among the people of the empire.

CHANGING THEOCRACIES

Sometimes a government shifts from one form of government to another. Today some theocratic governments are changing to democracies. Their citizens want more control over what their government does. They may protest in the streets to demand this change. If the country's leaders do not want to change the government, these protests can lead to war between the government and the people.

Mogadishu is the capital of Somalia. It is very poor, but its economy is improving after years of war.

From Theocracy to Democracy

A good example of a changing theocracy is Somalia. In 1976, the government of Somalia began to rule based on the laws of Islam. It gave the people very little freedom. The people also had little money to feed and shelter themselves.

In 1991, these problems lead to an ongoing civil war. Years of violence have nearly destroyed Somalia's economy. Many of its people are **refugees**. In 2004, the country began its change to democracy. And as of 2012, Somalia is a democratic country. It created democratic institutions, such as a president, a prime minister, and a parliament. The president is elected by the members of parliament. Islam remains the state religion. And the laws of Somalia continue to be based on sharia law. But the government is run by representatives of the people.

From Democracy to Theocracy

Sometimes a government changes from a democracy to a theocracy. The leaders often want to increase the power of their religion in their country. So they make the religion officially part of the government. This change often limits the citizens' freedoms, especially the freedom to follow their own religion.

Pakistan is a democracy but is moving toward theocracy. The government of Pakistan is ruled by both a president and a parliament. The citizens elect both. But the state religion of Islam is important in Pakistan. The constitution requires the president be a Muslim.

In 1980, the military group that ruled the government created the Federal Shariat Court. It wanted to increase the power of Islam within the government. This court reviews all laws to make sure they follow sharia law.

Pakistan's government is not a complete theocracy. But institutions such as the Federal Shariat Court increase the power of religion within the government.

Not a Muslim?

As Islam becomes more important in Pakistan's government, Pakistanis who practice religions other than Islam are in danger. They live in fear of violence from Islamic **extremists**. These people want to stop them from practicing their religion. The government is not protecting non-Muslims.

Muslim men and women pray in separate areas.

RIGHTS OF THE PEOPLE

The rights of the people under theocratic governments vary widely. Theocracy is often connected with totalitarian governments. In a totalitarian government, the government controls all aspects of life. These include politics, economy, culture, religion, and the private lives of citizens. In Saudi Arabia, Islam is seen as a way of life. There is no freedom of religion. The country forbids other religions from building places of worship.

Women's Rights in Theocracies

The Islamic government of Saudi Arabia and other Islamic governments limit the rights of women. Under sharia law, men have power over women. Many **human rights** organizations criticize how Islamic governments treat women. These governments deny women equal access to education, allow violence against women, and deny women equal rights.

In Saudi Arabia, women are not allowed out without a male guardian. Their testimony in court is worth only half that of a man's testimony. Women are not allowed to drive. Women's lack of rights under Islamic governments is a worldwide human rights issue.

Women in Saudi Arabia must eat in separate sections of a restaurant.

The citizens of Yemen voted in a presidential election in 2012.

Democratic Rights

But not all theocracies are totalitarian governments. Many theocracies are blended with forms of **representative democracy**. In these theocracies, citizens have more power and more rights. Because they can vote for their leaders, they can influence the government's decisions. They often vote for leaders who want to increase their freedoms and rights.

On the Arabian Peninsula, Yemen is a theocracy. Its laws are based on Islam's religious laws. But Yemen's government is a democracy. The president and the legislature are both elected by popular vote. Yemen was the first country in the Arabian Peninsula to allow women the right to vote.

But Islamic religious laws still limit the rights of Yemeni citizens. Yemeni women are often the victims of violence and discrimination. People who practice religions other than Islam are also discriminated against in Yemen.

Control by Religion

In totalitarian theocracies, governments use religion as one more way to control people. They use their faith to scare their citizens into cooperating with them. If a citizen disobeys the government, they risk not just their lives but their eternal lives. They also risk getting to live the **afterlife** they believe in.

THE ROLE OF CITIZENS

The roles citizens play in a theocracy vary widely. Because the laws of theocracies are based on religion, the first role of citizens is to follow the country's religion. Citizens who do not follow the state religion often have to hide their faith. Sometimes those citizens have to follow the laws of the religion anyway. For example, in Islam, people pray five times a day at specific times. When the time for prayer is called, all people must stop their work for the prayers, whether they are Muslim or not.

Following the State Religion

In Saudi Arabia, the government claims it allows citizens to practice any religion they want. But they must do so in private. The law does not protect publicly practicing a religion other than Islam. Non-Muslims must hide their faith or risk being arrested or **deported.** And no matter what citizens' religion are, they must follow sharia law while in Saudi Arabia.

Ninety-seven percent of Saudi Arabians are Muslim. The laws of the government are based on the laws of Islam. So no citizen can disagree with the laws of Saudi Arabia without disagreeing with the laws of Islam. Citizens find it difficult to criticize the government. If they do so, they are going against their religion.

In Islamic countries, a muezzin stands at the top of a **mosque.** He calls out five times a day to tell the people it is time to pray.

According to the prophet Zoroaster, Ahura Mazdā created the universe. Zoroastrians pray to him in Iran.

Limited Roles for Minorities

Some theocracies **tolerate** other religions. In Iran, the government protects a few religious **minorities**. It even reserves seats in the legislature for a certain number of minorities. But these minorities do not have the same role that Muslim citizens do. They cannot be president. They cannot even be the principal of a school. Though they can follow their religion, they are not equal to Muslim citizens. And much like in Saudi Arabia, all citizens are expected to follow the laws of Islam.

In democratic theocracies such as those in Yemen and Somalia, citizens take part directly in the political process. Their votes directly affect who rules the country. Citizens there are still expected to follow the laws of the state religion. However, they have more freedom in their personal lives.

People of the Book

The state religion of Iran is Islam. But the government also allows its citizens to practice **Zoroastrianism**, Judaism, and Christianity. These religions are allowed because they are based on the same religious books as Islam. Their followers are all "people of the book." Iran considers other religions to be against Islam's religious teachings so they are not allowed.

Often theocracies have one leader who is the head of the government and the head of the Church. The leader can be chosen politically, then become leader of the religion. Or the leader can be chosen religiously, then become leader of the government. Some theocracies use a combination of political and religious processes to choose their leaders.

The Political Process

Iran uses both elections and religious appointments to choose its leaders. Iran's government has a group of Islamic scholars called the Assembly of Experts. They use their religious knowledge to choose the Supreme Leader. The Supreme Leader of Iran holds the highest religious and political office in the country. But the members of the Assembly of Experts come to power through a political process. The people of Iran elect them.

The Assembly of Experts also has the power to remove the Supreme Leader.

Religious Ritual Finds the Leader

In central Asia, Tibet was an independent theocracy until it became part of China in 1951. Tibet's leader, called the dalai lama, was chosen based on religious traditions. The dalai lama was the highest religious official in the religion of Tibetan Buddhism. He was also the leader of the Tibetan government.

Tibetan Buddhists believe that when the previous dalai lama dies, he is **reincarnated** as a baby. He then grows up to be the new dalai lama. When a dalai lama dies, a group of important lamas, or monks, and the Tibetan government begin searching the country. They are looking for his reincarnation as a baby or young child. They use religious rituals to determine if a child is the new dalai lama. Once they find him, he leaves his home and trains to be the new leader of Tibet and Tibetan Buddhists.

The 13th Dalai Lama was the leader of the Tibetan Buddhist religion and the Tibetan government.

Elections in Iran

Even though Iran has elections, it is not a democracy. In a democracy, elections are free and fair. Elections in Iran are limited by the Guardian Council. The Guardian Council, part of the executive branch, must approve candidates before they can run for election. If a candidate suggests extreme changes to laws or the government, the council forbids that candidate from running. The people can only vote for candidates the Guardian Council approved.

The 14th Dalai Lama lives in India. He is not allowed to lead the Tibetan government.

LEADERS OF A THEOCRACY

Leaders in theocracies have varying amounts and kinds of power. Some leaders have complete control over the religion and the government. The power of other leaders depends on the support on their citizens. In some theocracies, the leader is in charge of the country but still must obey the laws of the religion. In other theocracies, the leader actually decides the rules of the religion.

King Louis XIV of France was known as "The Sun King." He ruled based on the divine right of kings.

The Divine Right of Kings

In **medieval** Europe, many kings claimed a right to rule. They based their right on an idea called "the divine right of kings." According to this theory, the king received his right to rule his people directly from God. He did not answer to anyone but God. He was not responsible to his people, other royal family members, or the Church. The king was not subject to the rules of religion, though he was the head of the religion.

Catholicism and King Louis XIV

King Louis XIV was a devout Catholic. He practiced his religion every day. During his rule, he made it difficult for anyone to practice any other religion. He closed many Protestant churches and did not let Protestants move freely around the country. Protestants were not allowed to hold political office or marry Catholics. But Protestants who became Catholics were rewarded financially.

Abd al-Rab Mansur Al-Hadi was elected president of Yemen in 2012.

Just Another Citizen

In democratic theocracies, the leader is an elected citizen. In Yemen, Somalia, and Afghanistan, the people elect presidents. However, the laws of these governments remain based on religion. These laws limit the power of the president, who must obey religious laws. The leader also has a limited term in office. Once his term is over, he may or may not run for re-election, depending on the laws of the country.

Head of the Church

The leader of Vatican City is the pope. He is also leader of the worldwide Catholic Church. His role as leader of the Church is more important than his role as leader of the government of Vatican City. The pope is the ultimate authority on all matters related to the Catholic Church. But he is still subject to the laws of that Church.

The role of the leader in a theocracy depends on the structure of the government. In some theocracies, the leader is an elected president who serves as the leader of the religion. In other theocracies, he is the most powerful religious leader who then leads the government.

25

Branches of Government

Every country's government works differently. However, the **federal,** or national, government is often divided into executive, legislative, and judicial branches.

Executive Branch

The executive branch is the branch of the leader. Executives include presidents, prime ministers, kings, and supreme leaders. This branch makes sure laws are obeyed. Executives in theocracies are chosen in various ways. Some inherit power, some are elected to their position, and some are appointed to their office. They all have a duty to enforce the laws of the government and the laws of the religion.

Legislative Branch

The legislative branch is responsible for making laws. Much like the executive branch, members of this branch get their jobs different ways. Some are appointed by the leader of the executive branch. Some are elected by the people.

The National Assembly of Afghanistan has two **houses**—the House of Elders and the House of People. The members of the House of People are elected by popular vote. The members of the House of Elders are appointed and elected. One-third of the members are appointed by the president. The other two-thirds are elected by members of the local and regional governments.

The Afghanistan parliament meets to debate laws and discuss issues with other leaders.

A judge in Yemen listens to arguments from a lawyer.

Judicial Branch

The final branch of government is the judicial branch. The judicial branch includes all the courts in the country. This branch is responsible for deciding whether the laws have been broken. In many modern theocracies, religion plays the greatest role in the judicial branch. Often the judges on the courts are religious scholars. They are appointed to their position based on their knowledge of religious law.

In Iran, the Supreme Leader appoints judges to the court. The judges make sure the laws passed by the legislative branch follow sharia law. They also preside over the country's civil and criminal courts. In these courts, they settle disputes between citizens and decide whether a citizen has broken the law. They also base these decisions on their knowledge of sharia law.

The Military

The military is usually part of the executive branch. It must follow the orders of the executive. A theocratic government may use its military to try to spread its religion. This is called a holy war. The military attacks people who practice a different religion to make them change faiths.

27

Most countries have three levels of government: federal, regional, and local. Regional and local governments are responsible for taking care of local problems. Some theocratic governments have more control over local governments than others. It depends on the country.

The number, power, and responsibilities of local governments vary depending on the theocracy. Larger countries require a larger number of local governments because there are more people spread over a larger geographical area. The more powerful the federal government is, the less power and fewer responsibilities the local governments will have. But the less powerful the federal government is, the more power and responsibilities local governments will have.

Afghanistan

Afghanistan is a theocracy in central Asia. The country is divided into 34 provinces. The president of Afghanistan appoints a governor for each province. Each province also has a provincial council, which is a group of local lawmakers. The people of the province elect the provincial council.

Sudan

The theocracy in Sudan is similar to the theocracy in Afghanistan. The country is divided into 26 states. Each of those states has a governor and a council of ministers. Unlike Afghanistan, the president appoints the council of ministers. He then chooses three candidates for governor. The people of the state then elect their governor from those choices. In Afghanistan and Sudan, members of the local governments represent the federal government.

Each of Afghanistan's provinces has its own capital and local government.

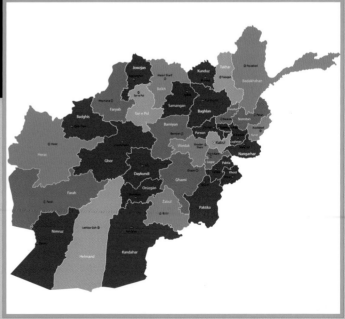

A group of tribal chieftains meets to discuss leadership issues in Yemen.

Local Powers

Local governments usually have limited power. They are responsible for taking care of the citizens in their geographic area. They cannot pass laws or enforce laws that would affect citizens outside their area. And they cannot pass or enforce laws that do not agree with the federal laws of the country. They are expected to follow the religious laws of the state religion.

Iran

In Iran, the people elect members of the local councils every four years. The local councils have many responsibilities. They elect mayors. They study the educational, health, and welfare needs of their people and try to fulfill those needs. They also figure out how the local cities and villages can carry out national laws.

Yemen

In Yemen, local governments have some independence from the federal government. The farther away from Yemen's capital an area is, the less control the federal government has over its people. In the rural areas of Yemen, local tribes run the government. They often act on their own authority. These governments are elected by the people.

COURTS AND THE LAW

When the legislative branch in a theocracy writes new laws, it must refer to the laws of its religion. Courts then make their decisions based on their understanding of these laws. In addition, some courts may also refer back to the religious texts themselves. Courts using the same texts may make different decisions based on their differing views of the religious text.

Iran: Following Sharia Law

Elected by the people, members of Iran's parliament write all the laws. But the Guardian Council has the final say over those laws. The Guardian Council is a group of 12 judges. Six of those judges are also religious officials. They review all laws passed by the parliament. They make sure the laws agree with sharia law. If the laws do not, the Guardian Council sends the law back to the parliament for rewriting. Iran's courts are then responsible for deciding whether someone has broken the laws.

Ayatollah Ahmad Jannati is the chairman of the Guardian Council in Iran. He was first elected to the council in 1980.

Lawyers argue cases every day in the General Court Building in Riyadh, Saudi Arabia.

A Matter of Personal Judgment

The laws and courts of Saudi Arabia are complex. Saudi Arabia uses the Quran and sharia law as its constitution. These documents were not written specifically to govern a country. So legislators and judges must base all their decisions on their own personal interpretations of sharia law. Each may have a slightly different interpretation.

The laws of Saudi Arabia come from several sources. One source is the decrees issued by the king. Another is the religious documents of Islam, including the Quran and the sayings and deeds of Muhammad. The Quran and the recorded sayings contain many **contradictions**. This situation forces judges to make personal judgments.

In the courts of Saudi Arabia, the judges must be members of the ulema—a group of Islamic religious leaders and scholars. Whatever decision the judge makes is final. There are no juries to hear the issues. The judges are often criticized for making harsh decisions. They are experts in sharia law. But their critics claim they do not know enough about modern life. For example, many judges interpret sharia law to ban video games and recorded music. These decisions limit citizens' freedom. But as long as a judge's decisions agree with sharia law, his judgments cannot be questioned.

Sharia Law

Sharia law is based on the work of the earliest Muslim scholars. It divides human acts into two categories, acts that people are allowed to do and acts that people are not allowed to do. It also lists punishments for specific crimes.

The role of business in a theocracy is also influenced by religion. In ancient theocracies, rulers used religion to organize their people. Faith rallied the people around a common cause. Once the people were organized, they were put to work for the good of the leader or the society.

In modern theocracies, the role of business depends on the form of the theocracy. Businesses may be owned by the government or by individuals.

Ancient Egypt

The society of ancient Egypt was well organized under the pharaoh. The people worked at farming, construction, religious studies, mining, medicine, and the military. Many government officials worked for the pharaoh. They organized the people's labor. They toiled together to create **irrigation** systems and build elaborate buildings. Ancient Egypt's ability to organize its people so well was due to its theocracy. The people believed their pharaoh was a god, so they were willing to cooperate and follow his plans.

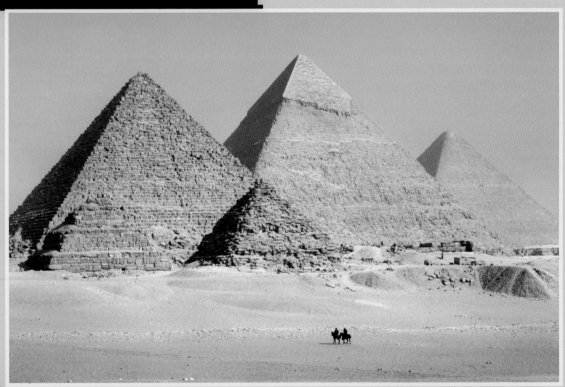

Ancient Egypt organized its people so well that they were able to build these huge pyramids in the desert.

The government-owned airline company ended at the beginning of the civil war. Now private companies provide air transportation.

Somalia and Growth

In a democratic theocracy such as Somalia, citizens own their businesses. Somalia had a civil war in the 1990s. Before then, the government owned many Somali businesses. The war, however, damaged must of the country's industry.

Since the war's end, Somali citizens who fled the country have been returning. They are investing their own money in the country's economy. Though the country is one of the poorest in the world, the economy has been growing steadily.

Holy Days and Business

Many religions have a certain day of the week they save for religious devotion. In theocratic countries, businesses often must close to respect these holy days. Islamic countries observe holy days on Fridays. Christian countries observe holy days on Sundays.

Saudi Arabia

In Saudi Arabia, the king is all-powerful. He controls the major industries in the country, including oil production. The majority of the country's economy is driven by this industry. Recently Saudi Arabia is in the process of selling government-owned businesses to private owners. The country hopes these new private owners will compete with each other to sell their goods and services. This competition will make the industry produce more and make more money.

Media are the organizations that spread news to the people. The media include newspapers, magazines, Internet news sites, and radio and television stations.

The role of the media in theocratic countries varies widely. The media may be controlled by the state or by private organizations. In some theocracies, the media is free to report on any topic. In other theocracies, the government owns the media and controls what they report. It works to make sure that what is reported agrees with the state religion.

Media and Censorship

The Saudi Arabian government tightly controls its media. The government does not support freedom of the press or freedom of speech. Citizens are not allowed to freely give their opinions. The media can only report stories that agree with the beliefs and principles of Islam, the state religion. They also cannot report stories that would cause citizens to rebel against the government or embarrass it. The government of Saudi Arabia allows citizens to read magazines and play video games, but only after it has **censored** them.

The only job of some Saudi officials is to review media. They delete anything that goes against the laws of Islam or criticizes the government.

Reporters for the Iranian media can only report on topics the government has approved.

In Iran, the media is a combination of government-owned and privately owned organizations. The laws and morals of Islam limit the subjects the media in Iran may cover. The government has the right to censor all media in the country. A special court is in charge of watching all the media. This court can cancel a newspaper's or television channel's license if it reports something that goes against the state religion of Islam. This includes a lot of North American and European television shows and movies.

Moving Toward a Free Press

Afghanistan has a history of government control of the media. But since 2002, this has been changing. The government has slowly relaxed its control of the press. Afghanistan's 2004 constitution goes so far as to ban censorship. It actively encourages freedom of the press. In practice, the media in Afghanistan is still subject to censorship. But the country is on a path to freedom of the press.

Freedom of the Press

Freedom of the press is the right of newspapers, magazines, radio shows, and other forms of media to report whatever they please. The government is not allowed to limit the stories covered by the media. Most democratic societies enjoy this freedom. But many theocratic governments limit freedom of the press to follow the laws of the state religion.

Role of Culture

In theocracies, nearly all the people in the country practice the state religion. Often the religion comes with customs and traditions. These have been passed down from **generation** to generation over hundreds of years. Religions influence people's beliefs, laws, and morals. In theocratic countries, where people all practice the same religion, the religion is the culture. Religion influences most art, literature, music, education, and people's private lives.

A Tibetan thangka, or wall hanging, shows the Buddha, who was the founder of Buddhism.

Tibetan Buddhism

Tibetan Buddhism is a religion practiced by people around the world. When China took over Tibet, Tibetan lamas, or monks, spread out all over the world to continue practicing and spreading their religion. Even though there is no longer a Tibetan Buddhist government, the religion continues to thrive.

Tibet

Tibetan Buddhism is a way of life. The art of the Tibetan people is deeply religious. It features paintings and weavings of Tibetan gods and other religious symbols. The music of Tibet is also based on Buddhism.

Women must wear an abaya, a long, black full-length covering in public in Saudi Arabia, They must also keep their hair covered.

Chanting is a popular form of music that comes from the religious tradition of repeating prayers. The people dress in long sleeves in the winter and the summer. This conservative dress also reflects their religious beliefs.

The Buddhist culture in Tibet helps unite its citizens. The people share the same beliefs and traditions, which are based on their religion. The religious culture also gives the people a shared system of right and wrong.

Saudi Arabia

In Saudi Arabia, Islam determines nearly everything in the people's lives. The religious beliefs of Muslims are in fact the laws of the country. Islam determines what the people eat, what they wear, and what they are allowed to do. It is illegal to sell pork and alcohol in the country because Islam forbids them. Islam requires modesty, so the people cover up their bodies as much as possible. Women conceal their entire bodies, their heads, and often their faces when they are in public. People pray five times a day when they hear the call to prayer from the local mosque. Whether people are Muslim or not, in Saudi Arabia, their daily life is ruled by the laws of Islam.

Forms of Government

	Democracy	Dictatorship
Basis of power	People elect officials to represent their views and beliefs.	The dictator controls everything in the country. His word is the law.
Rights of the people	People have many rights, including the right to fair and free elections, the right to assemble, and the right to choose how to live their lives.	The people have very few rights. Their duty is to do whatever the dictator wants.
How leaders are chosen	Frequent and regular elections are held to vote for leaders.	Leaders can inherit their position or take it with military force. The most powerful political party may also choose them.
Basis of judicial branch	A separate judicial branch enforces the laws made by the legislative branch. Laws are supposed to be enforced freely and fairly.	The judicial branch does what the dictator wants.
Relation of business to the form of government	Government plays a limited role in businesses. They may charge taxes and make some laws to make sure businesses are run fairly.	The government often owns the major businesses in a country.
Control of media	The government does not control the media. People have access to many opinions and diverse information from the media.	The dictator either tells the media what to report or censors the media's reports.
Role of religion	People may choose to practice their own religion.	People may or may not be able to practice their religion freely. However, political parties and focus on the dictator's personality are more important than religion.

Monarchy	Oligarchy	Theocracy
A monarch's power is inherited from a previous generation. In **absolute monarchies**, monarchs are believed to be chosen by God.	A select few use their wealth or secret connections to powerful people in the government to control the country. They are rarely elected.	The government is based on the state religion.
Rights are not guaranteed in an absolute monarchy. In a **constitutional monarchy**, rights are outlined in the country's constitution.	No rights are guaranteed, but in elected **oligarchies**, citizens can vote.	The laws of the state religion limit the rights of the people.
Power is passed down through families. Monarchies have different rules for who inherits power. In constitutional monarchies, the leaders of governing bodies, such as a parliament, are chosen through elections.	Oligarchs take power in most cases. They are rarely elected. They usually lead hidden behind the government.	Leaders are elected or appointed or chosen by religious customs.
In absolute monarchies, monarchs run the courts. Most constitutional monarchies have a separate judicial branch to ensure fair treatment.	Most oligarchies hide behind regular government functions. With their money and power, they affect the judicial branch's decisions.	All laws are based on the state religion. The judicial branch bases its judgments on that religion's laws.
Leaders of absolute monarchies control all of the wealth of a country. In constitutional monarchies, decisions about business are made by a governing body, such as a parliament.	Many oligarchs control wealthy businesses.	Businesses can be owned by citizens or by the government.
The press is not free in an absolute monarchy. Many constitutional monarchies, however, guarantee freedom of the media and speech.	Oligarchs tend to own and control all the media.	The media can be controlled by the government or by private citizens. It must follow the laws of the state religion.
Absolute monarchies often require people to have the same religion as the monarch. Many constitutional monarchies guarantee freedom of religion.	Some oligarchs share a common religion.	Religion forms the basis of the government. It dictates most aspects of the citizens' lives.

Assessing Theocracies

Here are some of the advantages of a theocracy.

- Theocracies give their citizens a sense of identity. Most citizens believe in the same religion, giving them a sense of shared culture. They know who they are and what they stand for.

- Theocracies unite their citizens. Most of the citizens believe in the same god and/or religious system. They will work together to serve that god.

- Theocratic governments also keep citizens under control. Citizens follow laws in a theocracy because they are the laws of their religion. They do not follow the laws just because the leader told them to. They follow them because they believe them deeply and believe their **eternal** lives depend on it.

Like previous Japanese emperors, Hirohito was thought to be chosen by God to rule. He used his connection to God to inspire the people of Japan during World War I.

Disadvantages to a Theocracy

Theocracies have some disadvantages, too.

- Often the laws of a theocracy's state religion limit the rights of its citizens. Citizens often cannot practice any religion other than their state religion. If they are allowed to practice another religion, they cannot do so in public.

- Whether citizens believe in the state religion or not, they still have to follow the laws of the religion. Those laws are the laws of the country.

- Many theocratic governments also limit freedom of speech and freedom of the press. The people are not allowed to say anything that goes against the state religion.

- Women in particular suffer in Islamic theocracies. Women have fewer rights than men and are often the subject of violence and discrimination. The laws of Islam support this, so they are unable to fight back.

- In a theocracy, it is more difficult to disagree with the government. If people want to change something about the way the government works, they seem to be arguing that the religion is wrong. Arguing against a religion is much more difficult than arguing against a government.

Citizens protest for their rights during the Arab Spring. The Arab Spring is a series of protests across the Islamic world against **oppressive** governments.

The Arab Spring

The Arab Spring is a series of protests throughout many Islamic nations. Protests have erupted in many Islamic countries, including Egypt, Tunisia, Libya, Yemen, Syria, Saudi Arabia, and Mauritania. The protests began in December 2010, and are ongoing. The citizens are demanding more freedom. Some want the right to vote. Others want elections to be free and fair, with a real choice among the candidates. And others are protesting against human rights abuses.

Theocratic governments ruled over people for thousands of years. In ancient theocracies, the leaders were believed to be gods. The people worshipped them and followed their orders. Over time, people stopped viewing their leaders as gods. The leader of a modern theocracy is often the head of the government as well as the highest official in the state religion. That leader is not, however, considered a god or divine.

Modern Theocracies

Theocracies can be based on any religion. But most theocracies today are based on Islam. Sharia law and the Quran form the basis for the laws of these countries.

Islam is also a way of life for the people in these nations. Practicing another religion is often discouraged or even illegal. In these theocracies, Islam influences everything from politics to the media to the food and dress of the people. And the citizens' belief in Islam helps unite them in their support of the government.

Challenges Facing Theocracies

In the past, theocracies brought people together by giving them a shared god and belief system. However, people today have greater access to the Internet. They are more likely to know about how other countries are run and governed. Increased **diversity** among a country's peoples also makes it more difficult to use just religion to keep people united.

As theocratic governments continue to rule, they will have to learn how to deal with the world changing around them. As their populations become more diverse, they will have to decide how to treat citizens who do not share the state religion. And as their citizens gain access to more information, they will have to figure out how to maintain control and unity. More people may begin to question their government and their religion.

Muslims practice their religion in mosques.

The challenge for theocratic governments will be to continue to unite and govern their citizens. They will have to do this even as fewer people follow the unifying force they have relied on for centuries—their shared religion.

Lamas practice Buddhism in the monastery in Lhasa, the capital of Tibet.

The first chapter of Yemen's constitution declares that the government of Yemen is an Arab Islamic state and that its laws are based on Islam.

Constitution of the Republic of Yemen

"Chapter I: The Political Foundations

"Article (I): The Republic of Yemen is an Arab, Islamic and independent **sovereign** state whose integrity is **inviolable**, and no part of which may be **ceded**. The people of Yemen are part of the Arab and Islamic Nation.

"Article (2): Islam is the religion of the state, and Arabic is its official Language.

"Article (3): Islamic (Sharia) is the source of all legislation.

"Article (4): The people of Yemen are the possessor and the source of power, which they exercise directly through public referendums and elections, or indirectly through the legislative, executive and judicial authorities, as well as through elected local councils.

"Article (5): The political system of the Republic of Yemen is based on political and partisan pluralism in order to achieve a peaceful transformation of power. The Law stipulates rules and procedures required for the formation of political organizations and parties, and the exercise of political activity. Misuse of Governmental posts and public funds for the special interest of a specific party or Political organization is not permitted."

YEMEN

As-Salif • SANA'A   Seiyun •   Al (Nisl

• Al Hudaydah   Sayhut

• Ibb   Al Mukalla   Arab

• Ta'izz   Soc

• Aden   Gulf of Aden

IND
OC

SOMALIA

Islam came to Yemen in the mid-600s CE and spread rapidly. Muhammad's son-in-law governed the area.

Somalia adopted a new constitution in 2012 as part of the country's change from theocracy to democracy.

Article 2. State and Religion

"(1) Islam is the religion of the State.

"(2) No religion other than Islam can be **propagated** in the country.

"(3) No law which is not **compliant** with the general principles and objectives of (Shariah) can be enacted.

Article 3. Founding Principles

"(1) The Constitution of the Federal Republic of Somalia is based on the foundations of the Holy Quran and the **Sunna** of our prophet Mohamed and protects the higher objectives of (Shariah) and social justice.

"(2) The Federal Republic of Somalia is a Muslim country which is a member of the African and Arab Nations.

"(3) The Federal Republic of Somalia is founded upon the fundamental principles of power sharing in a federal system...

"(5) Women must be included, in an effective way, in all national institutions, in particular all elected and appointed positions across the three branches of government and in national independent commissions."

In September 2012, Hassan Sheikh Mohamud was elected president. It was the first time in many years that a new president was chosen from inside Somalia.

GLOSSARY

absolute monarchies Governments in which rulers control every aspect of government. Rule is passed along family lines.

afterlife An existence after death

appointing Selecting someone for an office or job

Byzantine Empire A group of countries under a single ruler that formed in the early 300s CE after the fall of the Roman Empire. At one time, the Byzantine Empire included Greece, Italy, Egypt, Syria, North Africa, and southern Spain. The empire lasted for hundreds of years.

ceded Given up

censored Prevented publication or deleted ideas that cause offense or go against the government's views and goals

Christianity A religion that stresses belief in Jesus Christ and following his teachings

city-states Areas made up of a city and the surrounding area that govern themselves

civil war A war between groups of citizens of the same country

compliant In agreement

constitutional monarchy A system of government in which a king, queen, or sultan shares power usually with an elected government

contradictions Ideas that are opposite of each other

decrees Orders issued by a head of state that have the same impact as a law

deported Forced to leave a country

descendants People who come from a particular ancestor or group of ancestors

diversity Ways of being different; variety

edicts Laws or orders given by a ruler

eternal Existing forever without beginning or end; also refers to a belief in a life after death

extremists People who believe in ideas that are far beyond what is reasonable or normal

federal Describes the government group in charge of the whole country

generation Individuals who are one step in the line of descent of a family. A grandmother, mother, and daughter are three generations of a family.

houses Legislatures or other groups of lawmakers. Also known as chambers.

human rights Freedoms that are guaranteed for people because they are humans

institutions Organizations that are set up for specific reasons

interpretation An explanation of the meaning of something

inviolable Too sacred, or important, to be gone against

irrigation The act of bringing water to land

Islam A religion marked by belief in Allah as the only god, in Muhammad as his prophet, and in the Quran, a holy book

Jewish Describes followers of Judaism, a religion that stresses belief in one God and faithfulness to the laws of the Old Testament

medieval Referring to the Middle Ages, the period of European history from 500 to 1500 CE

minorities Parts of the population that differ from other groups in some ways and are often treated unfairly

mosque A place of worship for followers of Islam

Muslim Describes followers of Islam

oligarchies Governments in which a small group exercises control. Wealth and power is concentrated in just a few people's hands.

oppressive Describes control or rule by cruel or unfair means

Ottoman Empire A Muslim empire that stretched across the Middle East, southeastern Europe and North Africa from 1299 to 1923

propagated Spread out an idea or belief

prophets People who tell others that they have a message from a god or gods

refugees People who flee from a place to find safety

reincarnated Reborn in a new body or form

representative democracy A form of government in which a group of people is elected by a nation's citizens to form an independent ruling body

republic Government in which the authority and power belong to the people. They elect representatives to manage the government.

sovereign A person, group, or state having supreme power

Sunna The way of life based on the teachings of Muhammad

supernatural Beyond the natural world

tolerate To be able to put up with

Zoroastrianism a religion founded by the Persian prophet Zoroaster and marked by belief in a war between good and evil in the universe

FOR MORE INFORMATION

Books

Barnard, Bryn. *The Genius of Islam: How Muslims Made the Modern World.* New York: Knopf Books for Young Readers, 2011.

Richardson, Hazel, and Paul Challen. *Government in the Ancient World*, Life in the Ancient World. New York, NY: Crabtree Publishing, 2011.

DiPiazza, Francesca Davis. *Yemen in Pictures*, Visual Geography. Minneapolis, MN: Twenty-First Century Books, 2007.

Gray, Leon. *Iran*, Countries of the World. Washington, D.C.: National Geographic Society, 2008.

Tracy, Kathleen. *We Visit Saudi Arabia*, Your Land and My Land: The Middle East. Hockessin, DE: Mitchell Lane Publishers, 2011.

Websites

Academic Kids encyclopedia: www.academickids.com/encyclopedia/index.php/Theocracy

BBC Religions: Islam: www.bbc.co.uk/religion/religions/islam

Kids Past.Com: www.kidspast.com/world-history/0031-old-kingdom.php

Index